Journey of Faith Children's Curriculum

Part 1 - Receiving God's Revelation

&

Part 2 - Personal Relationship with God

Dr. Derrick L. Randolph Sr.

DEDICATION

I dedicate this book to my family, Sharon Randolph, Derrick L. Randolph Jr. and Joshua Isaiah Randolph

Journey of Faith Family Study Guide

Copyrighted Material

Copyright © 2019
Date of publication January 2019
Authored by Dr. Derrick Lamont Randolph Sr.
Published by Journey of Faith Ministries
Baltimore, Maryland
United States of America

Puzzles made at puzzle-maker.com

Biblical texts provided by www.biblegateway.com,

Which is operated by The Zondervan Corporation, L.L.C.

The character illustrations by Raina Ram and editing by Alina Cristea and Merissa Hann are works-for-hire.

All concepts, ideas, copy, sketches, art work, electronic files and other materials related to the Journey of Faith are the property of Journey of Faith Ministries.

Journey of Faith Ministries
contact@journeyoffaithministries.org
www.journeyoffaithministries.org

All rights reserved.
This book may not be reproduced in whole or in part by any process without written permission from the copyright holder.

ISBN-10:1-944166-12-2
ISBN-13:978-1-944166-12-0

Table of Contents

Introduction 6
Part 1 - Receiving God's Revelation 8
   Stage 1 - Learning about God 9
      Lesson #1 - God, the Creator 9
      Lesson #2 - God's power 13
      Lesson #3 - God's Authority 17
   Stage 2 - Knowing God 21
      Lesson #4 - God the Father 22
      Lesson #5 - Holy Spirit 25
      Lesson #6 - The power of Christ 29
      Lesson #7 - The Crucifixion I 31
      Lesson #8 - The Crucifixion II 34
      Lesson #9 - The Crucifixion III 37
      Lesson #10 – Faith 41
      Lesson #11 – Forgiveness 45
   Stage 4 - Life in God's Church 49
      Lesson #12 - The Church 50
      Lesson #13 - Baptism 53
      Lesson #14 - Last Supper 56
      Lesson #15 - Last Supper II 60
   Stage 5 - God's Scripture 63
      Lesson #16 - Sacred Scripture I 64
      Lesson #17 - Sacred Scripture II 68
Part II - Personal relationship with God 72
   Stage 6 - Walking in Grace 73
      Lesson #18 - Growing in grace 74

    Lesson #19 - Compassion for others 77
Stage 7 - Daily Deliverance.. 80
    Lesson #20 - Liberation... 81
    Lesson #21 – Rescued 84
    Lesson #22 - Saved for others' sake 87
    Lesson #23 - "Restored".. 90
Stage 8 - Developing Discipline... 93
    Lesson #24 - "Fasting & Prayer" 94
    Lesson #25 - "Praise & Worship".. 98
    Lesson #26 - "Service & Fellowship" 102
Stage 9 - Loving obedience.. 106
    Lesson #27 - Love I... 107
    Lesson #28 - Love II 110
    Lesson #29 - Obedience 112
Stage 10 - Suffering Affliction 116
    Lesson #30 - Suffering.. 117
    Lesson #31 - Maturity & Resilience 121
Stage 11 – Glory.. 125
    Lesson #32 - The Glory of God 126
    Lesson #33 - Christ formed in you 130

Introduction

I have outlined the Journey of Faith, using the ascent and descent of Mount Sinai. As we go up, we navigate through the process of spiritual development where we are receiving God's revelation. As we go down Mount Sinai, we are developing a personal relationship with God.

There are various stages along the journey and lessons to walk through. The Journey of Faith Children's Curriculum features:

- Bible Story *(NIV)*
- Children's Chat *(short lesson to help children discuss and retell the story)*
- Fun Activity (Crossword Puzzle or Word Search)
- Prayers and poems

We wish God's grace and peace to you. We hope you are blessed by the Journey of Faith. Here are the Instructions

1. Read the **Bible Story** together *(NIV)*.
2. Allow the children to start the **Children's Chat** (ages 10 and under).
3. Use the answer key to review and discuss the **Children's Chat**.
4. Allow the children to complete the **Fun Activity** independently.
5. Review the **Fun Activity** together.
6. Read the **Prayers**, and **Poems** aloud together.

Journey of Faith Family Study Guide

Part 1 - Receiving God's Revelation

"The Season of Learning"

Journey of Faith Family Study Guide

Stage 1 - Learning about God

Lesson #1 - God, the Creator

Bible Story

Then God said, "Let us make mankind in our image, in our likeness, so that they may rule over the fish in the sea and the birds in the sky, over the livestock and all the wild animals, and over all the creatures that move along the ground." So God created mankind in his own image, in the image of God he created them; male and female he created them. (Genesis 1:26-27 NIV)

Journey of Faith Family Study Guide

Children's Chat

1. *Who were the people involved in the story?*

   _____
   _____
   _____
   _____

2. *What happened in the story?*

   God decided to _ _ _ _ mankind in the _ _ _ _ _ _ of God.

   God wanted man to_ _ _ _ over the animals.

   _ _ _ created _ _ _ _ _ _ _ _.

   God created man and _ _ _ _ _.

3. *What does this story teach us about ourselves? God?*

   _____
   _____
   _____
   _____
   _____
   _____
   _____

Poem

God, created the world, sun, moon and stars, Grass, flowers and trees
God put the ideas in our minds to create cars and boats that sail the seas

God created Sharks, turtles, flies and bumble bees
Things we like and things we don't, but God made them as He pleased

God created us and then created us to reign
To live within our purpose, we should operate the same

Men and women must rule
That's God's expectation
Created by God and called to
Rule Over the rest of creation

Caring for, protecting it,
Being responsible for them
Not destroying it,
But prolonging life that lives within

God created the creatures, but also the planet.
We live on it, and care for it. It's ours to manage.

Prayer

God create in us a heightened awareness of your presence

Journey of Faith Family Study Guide

Fun Activity

Lesson #2 - God's power

Bible Story

God blessed them and said to them, "Be fruitful and increase in number; fill the earth and subdue it. Rule over the fish in the sea and the birds in the sky and over every living creature that moves on the ground." Then God said, "I give you every seed-bearing plant on the face of the whole earth and every tree that has fruit with seed in it. They will be yours for food. And to all the beasts of the earth and all the birds in the sky and all the creatures that move along the ground—everything that has the breath of life in it—I give every green plant for food." And it was so. God saw all that he had made, and it was very good. And there was evening, and there was morning—the sixth day. (Genesis 1:28-31 NIV)

Children's Chat

i. *Who were the people in your story?*

_____

_____

_____

_____

ii. *What happened in your story?*

God _ _ _ _ _ _ _ them.

God told them how to _ _ _ _.

God said that He gave the _ _ _ _ _ _, _ _ _ _ _, and _ _ _ _ _ _ _ _ _ for food.

God looked at His _ _ _ _ _ _ _ _ and called it _ _ _ _.

iii. *Is there a promise of God discussed?*

God promised them _ _ _ _.

iv. *What are we being told to do?*

We are told to be _ _ _ _ _ _ _ _

We are told to _ _ _ _ _ _ _ _.

Fill and _ _ _ _ _ _ the earth

Rule over _ _ _ _ _ _ _ _ _.

v. *What does this story teach us about ourselves? God?*

This story teaches us to enjoy _____

Poem

Your God has power
God can do what he wants and He has the power carry it out

He created the world by His might
God has the past, present and future all at once in sight

God created people and the situations we live in
We need to know the God of our situations while we are in them.

Knowing God as creator means knowing who made me
Knowing who owns me, and who will step in and save me!

Here is a truth to savor.
He alone is our creator!

Prayer

God make us more like you. Share your spirit with us and let us learn to create opportunities to love like you.

Journey of Faith Family Study Guide

Fun Activity

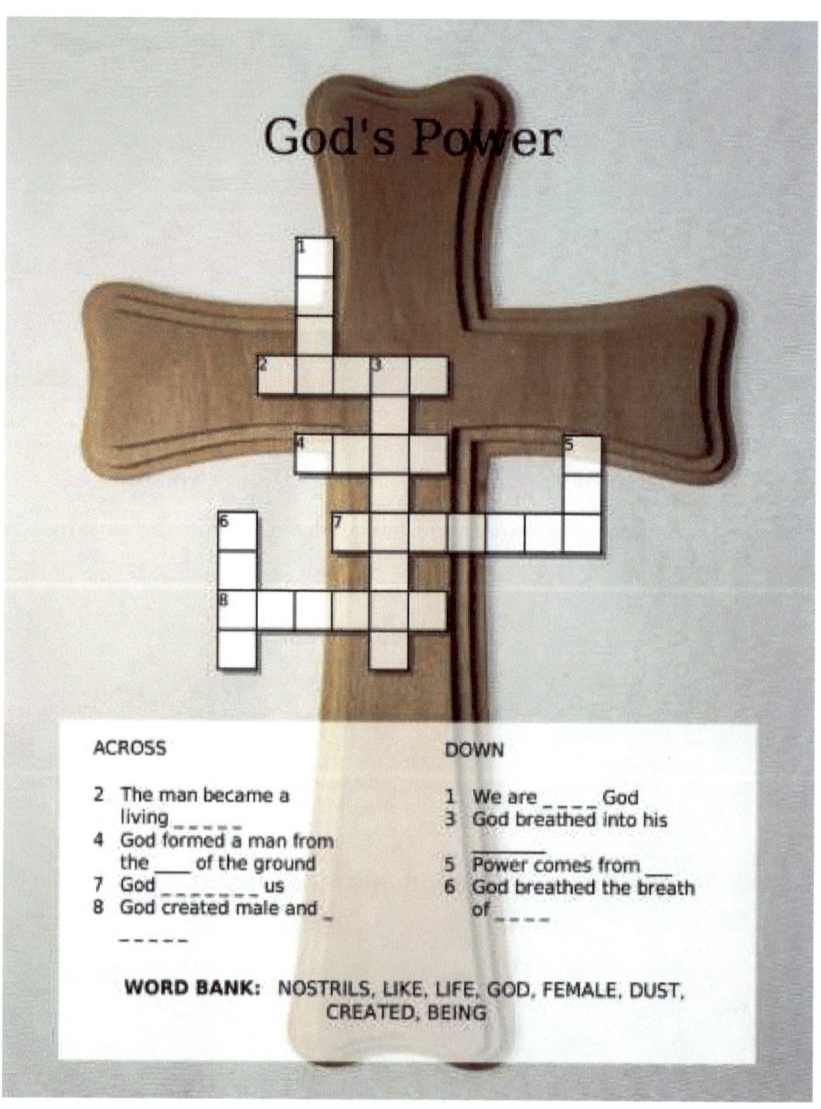

ACROSS
2. The man became a living _ _ _ _ _
4. God formed a man from the ___ of the ground
7. God _ _ _ _ _ _ _ us
8. God created male and _ _ _ _ _ _

DOWN
1. We are _ _ _ _ God
3. God breathed into his ___
5. Power comes from ___
6. God breathed the breath of _ _ _ _

WORD BANK: NOSTRILS, LIKE, LIFE, GOD, FEMALE, DUST, CREATED, BEING

Lesson #3 - God's Authority

Bible Story

Let everyone be subject to the governing authorities, for there is no authority except that which God has established. The authorities that exist have been established by God. Consequently, whoever rebels against the authority is rebelling against what God has instituted, and those who do so will bring judgment on themselves. For rulers hold no terror for those who do right, but for those who do wrong. Do you want to be free from fear of the one in authority? Then do what is right and you will be commended. For the one in authority is God's servant for your good. But if you do wrong, be afraid, for rulers do not bear the sword for no reason. They are God's servants, agents of wrath to bring punishment on the wrongdoer. Therefore, it is necessary to submit to the authorities, not only because of possible punishment but also as a matter of conscience. (Romans 13:1-5 NIV)

Journey of Faith Family Study Guide

Children's Chat

i. *Who is the writer of the passage?*

_____

_____

_____

_____

ii. *What act of obedience is demanded?*

We are told to _ _ _ _ the _ _ _ _ _ _ _ _ _ _ _.

iii. *Is there a promise of God discussed?*

God promises that if you do what is right, you will be _____.

God promises that rebellion against authority is rebellion against

_____

God promises that rebellion will bring judgment on _____.

iv. *What does this story teach us about God?*

This story teaches that only <u>God</u> has _____.

Poem

Let us obey those that lead

For, it's really to God that we heed.

God appointed them,

God anointed them

God chose them, not us

There's nothing left to discuss.

They are an extension of our God,

Disobey! Rise up and fight, and your opponent will be God.

Recognize your God in whomever He uses

Surrender to your God and obey!

There are no excuses,

It's your love for God on display.

It is better to be showered by God's love,

What a horror it would be,

To be slaughtered by God's wrath

Because you don't recognize His authority!

Journey of Faith Family Study Guide

Fun Activity

God's Authority

ACROSS

3 The person in authority is God's _____ for your good
4 people ____ against authority
6 God _____ the events of our lives

DOWN

1 we bring _____ on ourselves
2 God put people in authority
5 people should ____ to authority

WORD BANK: SUBMIT, SOMETIMES, SERVANT, JUDGMENT, DIRECTS, AUTHORITY

Journey of Faith Family Study Guide

Stage 2 - Knowing God

Journey of Faith Family Study Guide

Lesson #4 - God the Father

Bible Story

Since ancient times no one has heard, no ear has perceived, no eye has seen any God besides you, who acts on behalf of those who wait for him. You come to the help of those who gladly do right, who remember your ways. But when we continued to sin against them, you were angry. How then can we be saved? All of us have become like one who is unclean, and all our righteous acts are like filthy rags; we all shrivel up like a leaf, and like the wind our sins sweep us away. No one calls on your name or strives to lay hold of you; for you have hidden your face from us and have given us over to our sins. Yet you, LORD, are our Father. We are the clay, you are the potter; we are all the work of your hand. (Isaiah 64:4-9)

Journey of Faith Family Study Guide

Children's Chat

i. *Who is the writer of the passage?* _____

_____

_____

ii. *Is sin discussed? What about it? What sin?*

_____

Yes, sin is discussed. We all _ _ _. No one _ _ _ _ _ on _ _ _ or _ _ _ _ _ _ _ for God as they should.

iii. *Is there a promise of God discussed?*

_____

There is a promise that God acts on. It is for those who _ _ _ _ for him.

God helps those who do _ _ _ _ _. There is a promise that God gets _ _ _ _ _ when we sin against God's ways.

iv. *What does this story teach us about ourselves? God?* -

_____

This story teaches us that no one has _ _ _ _ _, perceived, or _ _ _ _ any other God. God is our Father. He is the _ _ _ _ _ _. We are _ _ _ _ in His hands.

Prayer

Lord, teach us to know you, and recognize your ways. Teach us to search for you with our hearts and desire to please you. Let us be shaped by you. Then we will belong to you. Amen

Journey of Faith Family Study Guide

Fun Activity

God The Father

ACROSS

4. The LORD has _____ on those who fear him
6. We are the clay, you are the _____
7. God _____ us deeply
8. When we sin against God, we _____ Him

DOWN

1. God is like a parent and we are His _____
2. we are all the work of your _____
3. How then can we be _____?
5. We owe God the highest love, reverence and _____
9. All our righteous acts are like filthy _____

WORD BANK: SAVED, RAGS, POTTER, OBEDIENCE, LOVES, HAND, COMPASSION, CHILDREN, ANGER

Journey of Faith Family Study Guide

Lesson #5 - Holy Spirit

Bible Story

When the day of Pentecost came, they were all together in one place. Suddenly a sound like the blowing of a violent wind came from heaven and filled the whole house where they were sitting. They saw what seemed to be tongues of fire that separated and came to rest on each of them. All of them were filled with the Holy Spirit and began to speak in other tongues as the Spirit enabled them. Now there were staying in Jerusalem God-fearing Jews from every nation under heaven. When they heard this sound, a crowd came together in bewilderment, because each one heard their own language being spoken. Utterly amazed, they asked: "Aren't all these who are speaking Galileans? Then how is it that each of us hears them in our native language? Parthians, Medes and Elamites; residents of Mesopotamia, Judea and Cappadocia, Pontus and Asia, Phrygia and Pamphylia, Egypt and the parts of Libya near Cyrene; visitors from Rome (both Jews and converts to Judaism); Cretans and Arabs—we hear them declaring the wonders of God in our own tongues!" Amazed and perplexed, they asked one another, "What does this mean?" Some, however, made fun of them and said, "They have had too much wine." (Acts 2:1-13 NIV)

Journey of Faith Family Study Guide

Children's Chat

i. *Who were the people in your story?*

_____

_____

_____

ii. *When and where did this story take place?*

The story took place on the day of _____ in Jerusalem in the _____ _____.

iii. *What happened in your story?*

A sound _____ the house and tongues of _____ rested on each of them. They were filled with the _____ _____ and began to speak in other tongues. A _____ came together and asked "What does this mean?" The crowd made _____ of them and said, "They have had too much wine."

iv. *What does this story teach us about ourselves? God?*

God's spirit led them to declare the wonders of _____ in others native tongues.

Poem

Oh mighty wind of Pentecost,
We wait on you at great cost!

To be filled, with tongues of fire
Oh mighty wind take our spirits higher

To speak in words unknown to me, or in words unknown to all
Oh mighty it's time to fall!

Fall afresh on us oh wind,
Fall and let it have no end

Fall, we are on one accord
Make unto us a threefold chord

Oh mighty wind, Spirit of God,
Burn our flesh until it's charred

Oh mighty wind,
Our God that flies, purify, purify!
Oh mighty wind we wait for you.
We need your power, we need you!

Journey of Faith Family Study Guide

Fun Activity

Holy Spirit

ACROSS
3. The Holy Spirit is sent forth from the _____ through the Son
4. We _____ the wonders of God
5. The Holy Spirit perfects the _____ given through the Son
7. The Holy Spirit brings us _____

DOWN
1. The Holy Spirit helps us do the _____ of God
2. The Holy Spirit sanctifies and _____ the saints
6. The Holy Spirit brings us on one _____

WORD BANK: WORKS, TOGETHER, SALVATION, PROCLAIM, GLORIFIES, FATHER, ACCORD

Journey of Faith Family Study Guide

Lesson #6 - The power of Christ

Bible Story

Then Peter stood up with the Eleven, raised his voice and addressed the crowd: "Fellow Jews and all of you who live in Jerusalem, let me explain this to you; listen carefully to what I say. These people are not drunk, as you suppose. It's only nine in the morning! No, this is what was spoken by the prophet Joel: 'In the last days, God says, I will pour out my Spirit on all people. Your sons and daughters will prophesy, your young men will see visions, your old men will dream dreams. Even on my servants, both men and women, I will pour out my Spirit in those days, and they will prophesy. I will show wonders in the heavens above and signs on the earth below, blood and fire and billows of smoke. The sun will be turned to darkness and the moon to blood before the coming of the great and glorious day of the Lord. And everyone who calls on the name of the Lord will be saved.' (Acts 2:14-21 NIV)

Journey of Faith Family Study Guide

Children's Chat

i. *Who were the people involved in your story?*

_____

_____

_____

ii. *What happened in your story?*

Then _ _ _ _ _ stood up with the Eleven, raised his voice and addressed the crowd

'In the last days, God says, I will pour out my _ _ _ _ _ _ on all people. Your sons and daughters will _ _ _ _ _ _ _ _, your young men will see _ _ _ _ _ _ _, your old men will dream _ _ _ _ _ _.

I will show _ _ _ _ _ _ _ in the heavens above and _ _ _ _ _ on the earth below.

And everyone who calls on the name of the _ _ _ _ will be _ _ _ _ _.

iii. *Is there a promise of God discussed?*

_____

_____

_____

iv. *What does this story teach us about ourselves? God?*

It teaches us that God has plans for His _____. We will all experience the _____ of God and receive revelation from God.

Lesson #7 - The Crucifixion I

Bible Story

As they were going out, they met a man from Cyrene, named Simon, and they forced him to carry the cross. They came to a place called Golgotha (which means "the place of the skull"). There they offered Jesus wine to drink, mixed with gall; but after tasting it, he refused to drink it. When they had crucified him, they divided up his clothes by casting lots. And sitting down, they kept watch over him there. Above his head they placed the written charge against him: This is Jesus, The King of the Jews. (Matthew 27:32-38 NIV)

Children's Chat

i. *Who were the people in your story?*

_____

_____

ii. *What happened in your story?*

The soldiers forced _____ to carry the cross for Jesus.

They crucified Jesus at _____.

They offered Jesus _____, but he refused to drink it.

iii. *What act of sin is discussed?*

They cast lots for his _____ and watched him there.

_____ and _____ Jesus was an act of sin, showing their disbelief in Jesus as the Son of God.

iv. *What does this story teach us about ourselves? God?*

This story teaches us that while the _____ mocked Jesus and were irreverent towards God, Simon of Cyrene _____ for Jesus. This act symbolizes the fact that all followers, disciples of Jesus must carry their own _____ for Jesus.

Prayer

Lord, every time we see the cross, remind us that it requires a lifetime of faithful love and service in honor of Jesus and obedience to the will of God. Amen!

Journey of Faith Family Study Guide

Fun Activity

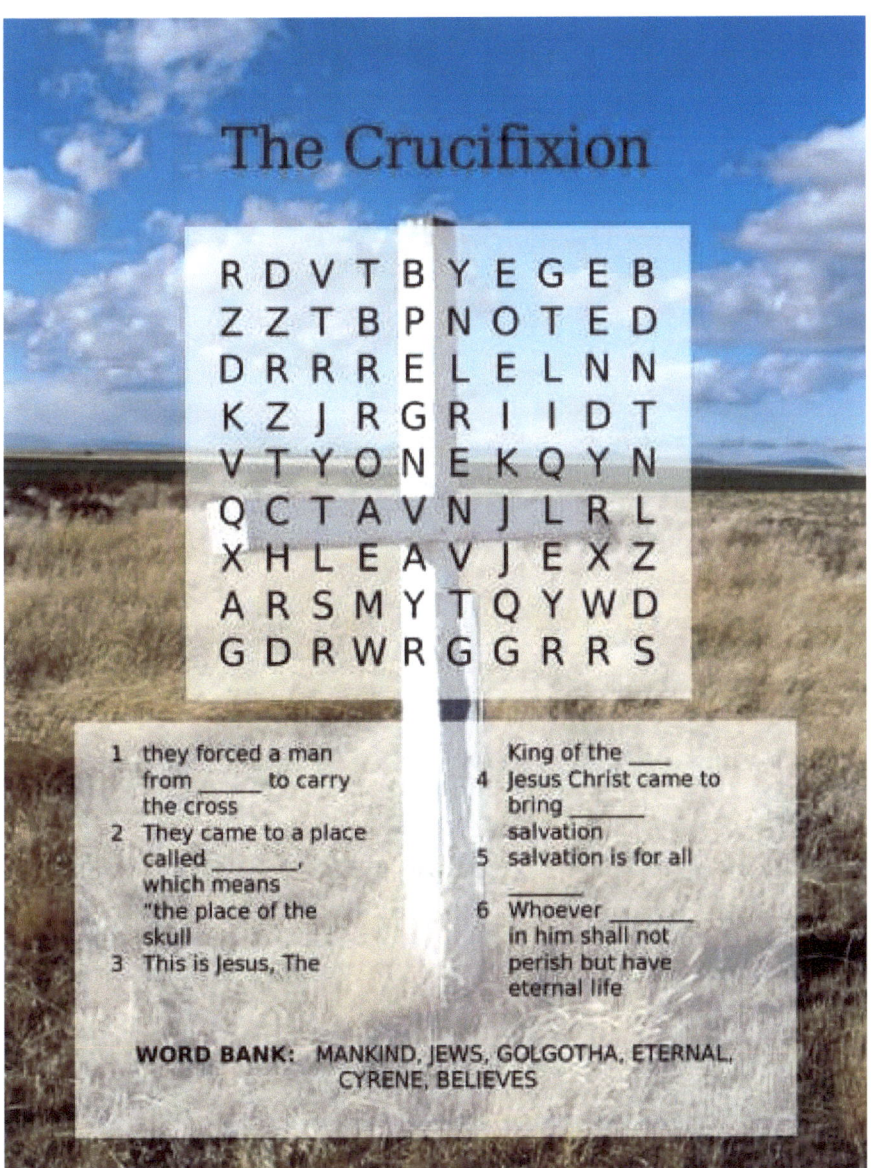

The Crucifixion

```
R D V T B Y E G E B
Z Z T B P N O T E D
D R R R E L E L N N
K Z J R G R I I D T
V T Y O N E K Q Y N
Q C T A V N J L R L
X H L E A V J E X Z
A R S M Y T Q Y W D
G D R W R G G R R S
```

1. they forced a man from _____ to carry the cross
2. They came to a place called _____, which means "the place of the skull
3. This is Jesus, The _____ King of the _____
4. Jesus Christ came to bring _____ salvation
5. salvation is for all _____
6. Whoever _____ in him shall not perish but have eternal life

WORD BANK: MANKIND, JEWS, GOLGOTHA, ETERNAL, CYRENE, BELIEVES

Journey of Faith Family Study Guide

Lesson #8 - The Crucifixion II

Bible Story

Two rebels were crucified with him, one on his right and one on his left. Those who passed by hurled insults at him, shaking their heads and saying, "You who are going to destroy the temple and build it in three days, save yourself! Come down from the cross, if you are the Son of God!" In the same way the chief priests, the teachers of the law and the elders mocked him. "He saved others," they said, "but he can't save himself! He's the king of Israel! Let him come down now from the cross, and we will believe in him. He trusts in God. Let God rescue him now if he wants him, for he said, 'I am the Son of God.'" In the same way the rebels who were crucified with him also heaped insults on him. (Matthew 27:38-44 NIV)

Children's Chat

i. *Who were the people in your story?*

   _____

ii. *What happened in your story?*

   People _____ and mocked _____, and told him to come down from the _____.

iii. *What act of sin is discussed?*

   The sin discussed in this story is that none of the people <u>trusted</u> in Jesus. They wanted to see a _____ instead.

iv. *What does this story teach us about ourselves? God?*

   This story teaches us that God requires us to have _____. We must learn to trust _____ even when our path seems dark.

<u>*Poem*</u>

Two men crucified,
One on each side

No one believes or trusts God.
There is no faith!
No one loves God
Only insults, just hate!

He endured hammers, nails, blood and death,
Taking His very last breath

He suffered knowing we didn't believe in Him,
Yet he saved us from our sins!
On the cross!

Journey of Faith Family Study Guide

Fun Activity

Journey of Faith Family Study Guide

Lesson #9 - The Crucifixion III

Bible Story

From noon until three in the afternoon darkness came over all the land. About three in the afternoon Jesus cried out in a loud voice, *"Eli, Eli, lema sabachthani?"* (Which means "My God, my God, why have you forsaken me?"). When some of those standing there heard this, they said, "He's calling Elijah." Immediately one of them ran and got a sponge. He filled it with wine vinegar, put it on a staff, and offered it to Jesus to drink. The rest said, "Now leave him alone. Let's see if Elijah comes to save him." And when Jesus had cried out again in a loud voice, he gave up his spirit. At that moment the curtain of the temple was torn in two from top to bottom. The earth shook, the rocks split and the tombs broke open. The bodies of many holy people who had died were raised to life. They came out of the tombs after Jesus' resurrection and went into the holy city and appeared to many people. When the centurion and those with him who were guarding Jesus saw the earthquake and all that had happened, they were terrified, and exclaimed, "Surely he was the Son of God!" Many women were there, watching from a distance. They had followed Jesus from Galilee to care for his needs. (Matthew 27:45-55 NIV)

Journey of Faith Family Study Guide

Children's Chat

i. *Who were the people in your story?*

_____

_____

ii. *What happened in your story*

_____ came over all the land.

Jesus cried out in a loud voice, "My God, my God, why have you _____ me?"

Someone offered a _____ to Jesus to drink.

When Jesus had cried out again in a loud voice, he gave up his _____.

The _____ of the temple was torn in two from top to bottom.

The earth _____, the rocks split and the tombs broke open.

The bodies of many holy people who had _____ were raised to life.

They came out of the _____ after Jesus' _____ and went into the holy city and appeared to many people.

They were terrified, and exclaimed, "Surely he was the Son of _____!"

The women _____ for his needs.

iii. *What act of obedience is discussed?*

Jesus _____ on the cross was an act of obedience.

iv. *What does this story teach us about ourselves? God?*

This story teaches us that Jesus preached liberty to the _____ and they rose again just as Jesus did at His _____. The darkness, the shaking earth, temple torn in _____ all signified that God had turned away from this painful event, and that God's will was _____.

Journey of Faith Family Study Guide

Prayer

Lord, let us learn to trust in you
We suffer when we're going through

Lord, let the spirit lead us to
The destination designed by you

That's what Jesus died to do
Share His spirit, comfort too

The curtain was torn in two
So that we may come to you

Bodies rose, Jesus rose
We will rise, now we know

We'll walk the step, of the master
He said greater will come after

Greater things we will do
But the Spirit makes lives brand new

We will help win the lost
Because there is power in the cross

Journey of Faith Family Study Guide

Fun Activity

Lesson #10 – Faith

Bible Story

While he was saying this, a synagogue leader came and knelt before him and said, "My daughter has just died. But come and put your hand on her, and she will live." Jesus got up and went with him, and so did his disciples. Just then a woman who had been subject to bleeding for twelve years came up behind him and touched the edge of his cloak. She said to herself, "If I only touch his cloak, I will be healed." Jesus turned and saw her. "Take heart, daughter," he said, "your faith has healed you." And the woman was healed at that moment. When Jesus entered the synagogue leader's house and saw the noisy crowd and people playing pipes, he said, "Go away. The girl is not dead but asleep." But they laughed at him. After the crowd had been put outside, he went in and took the girl by the hand, and she got up. News of this spread through all that region. (Matthew 9:18-26 NIV)

Children's Chat

i. *Who were the people in your story?*

_____

_____

_____

_____

i. *What act of obedience is discussed?*

The synagogue leader asked Jesus to come save his _____. Jesus went, but on the way, a woman touched the edge of his _____. She was _____ Jesus went to the synagogue leader's house and _____ the girl back to _____.

The synagogue leader and the woman that was bleeding both had faith in Jesus and acted on their faith.

ii. *Was there a difficult decision to make? If so, what?*

The Synagogue _____ and the woman both had the difficult decision of publicly expressing their need for Jesus' _____.

iii. *Is there a promise of God discussed?*

Jesus shared a truth with the woman that is still true, a promise for us today. Our faith [in Jesus] will _____ us.

iv. *What are we being told to do?*

Jesus wants us to act in _____.

v. *What does this story teach us about ourselves? God?*

The story teaches us that Jesus is available to help us, if we _____ by faith that Jesus will do it.

Prayer

Lord teach us to see the impossible, remember that you can do it and believe that you will do it.

Journey of Faith Family Study Guide

Fun Activity

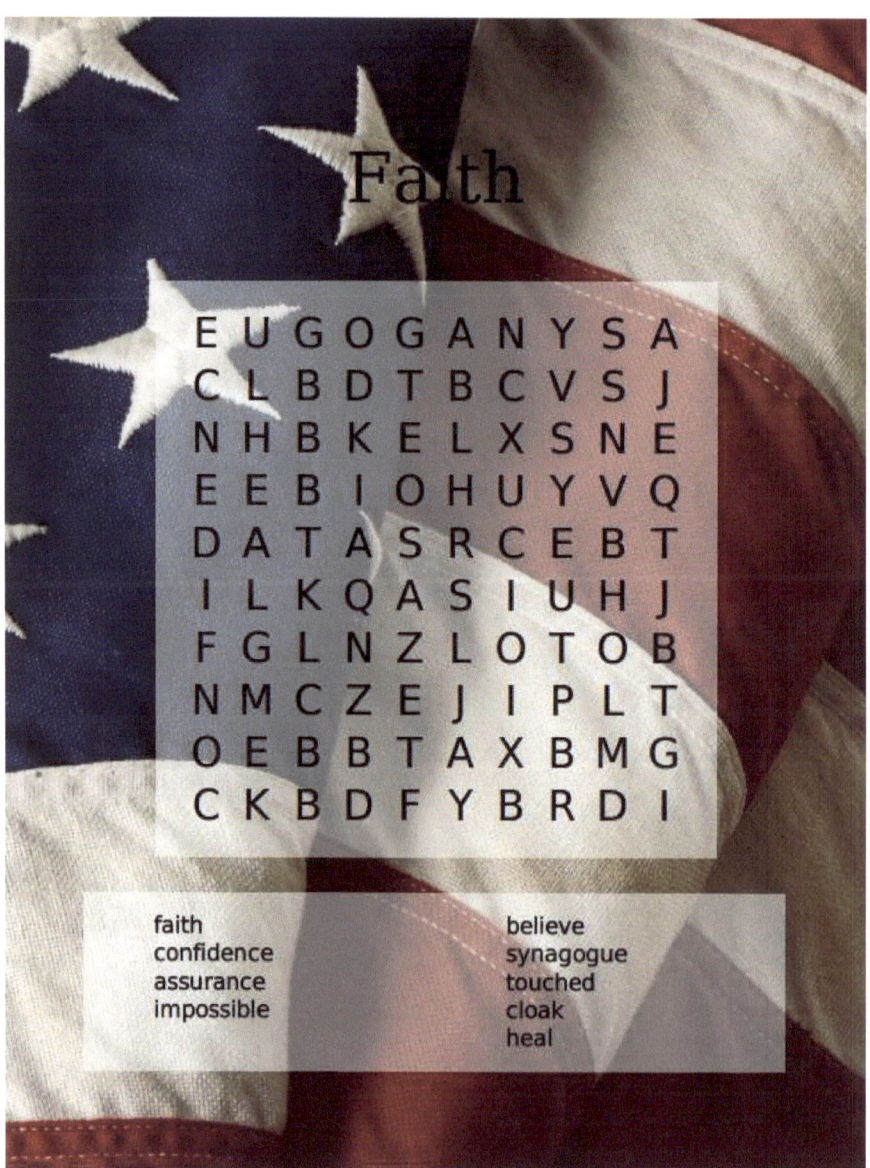

Journey of Faith Family Study Guide

<u>Lesson #11 – Forgiveness</u>

Bible Story

Then Peter came to Jesus and asked, "Lord, how many times shall I forgive my brother or sister who sins against me? Up to seven times?" Jesus answered, "I tell you, not seven times, but seventy-seven times. "Therefore, the kingdom of heaven is like a king who wanted to settle accounts with his servants. As he began the settlement, a man who owed him ten thousand bags of gold was brought to him. Since he was not able to pay, the master ordered that he and his wife and his children and all that he had be sold to repay the debt.

"At this the servant fell on his knees before him. 'Be patient with me,' he begged, 'and I will pay back everything.' The servant's master took pity on him, canceled the debt and let him go. "But when that servant went out, he found one of his fellow servants who owed him a hundred silver coins. He grabbed him and began to choke him. 'Pay back what you owe me!' he demanded. "His fellow servant fell to his knees and begged him, 'Be patient with me, and I will pay it back.' "But he refused. Instead, he went off and had the man thrown into prison until he could pay the debt. When the other servants saw what had happened, they were outraged and went and told their master everything that had happened. "Then the master called the servant in. 'You wicked servant,' he said, 'I canceled all that debt of yours because you begged me to. Shouldn't you have had mercy on your fellow servant just as I had on you?' In anger his master handed him over to the jailers to be tortured, until he should pay back all he owed. (Matthew 18:21-34 NIV)

Children's Chat

i. *Who were the people in your story?*

_____

_____

_____

_____

ii. *What happened in your story?*

Peter asked Jesus how many times to forgive someone who _____ against you. Jesus answered _____ times. Jesus told a _____ about the kingdom of _____ where a king forgave a _____ who did not forgive one of his fellow servants so his master handed him over to the _____ to be _____, until he paid back all he owed.

iii. *What act of sin is discussed?*

The servant sinned by not extending forgiveness, especially after he was just granted forgiveness of his debt by his _____.

iv. *What does this story teach us about ourselves?*

We should have _____ on our brother or sister who sins against us, just as the Lord has had sin on us.

v. *What does this story teach us about God?*

This story teaches us that God is _____ and merciful toward _____, but God is also just (fair). God expects us to _____ others the way God treats us.

Poem

We wrestle with these questions,
Though we know the truth
Our daily encounters become routine lessons,
And the answers become absolutes.
Etched in our hearts after the hundredth time
That we fail to forgive, we are stuck on rewind.
Should we forgive? Can we forgive? Why should I forgive him or her?
How often should I forgive? How many times should I forgive someone that does not deserve?

For, if God forgives, you should forgive!
If you don't, then He won't either.
Expect an endless cycle of pain, you will never get a breather!

If you forgive, then God will lift the weight off of your heart
The little bit of hate you held was tearing your apart.

Forgiveness builds relationships, forgiving is demanding
You start out with an acquaintanceship that takes flight and comes down for a landing.
Your status as friends is up in the air, then when you are forced to forgive
You begin to invest in a person, and your relationship begins to live.
Forgiveness is hard work, it's very difficult at times.
It makes you faithful, sincere, holy down inside.

Who can have a patient heart that forgives man's frequent wrongs?
That's the one who forgives and quietly lives right with God?

Journey of Faith Family Study Guide

Fun Activity

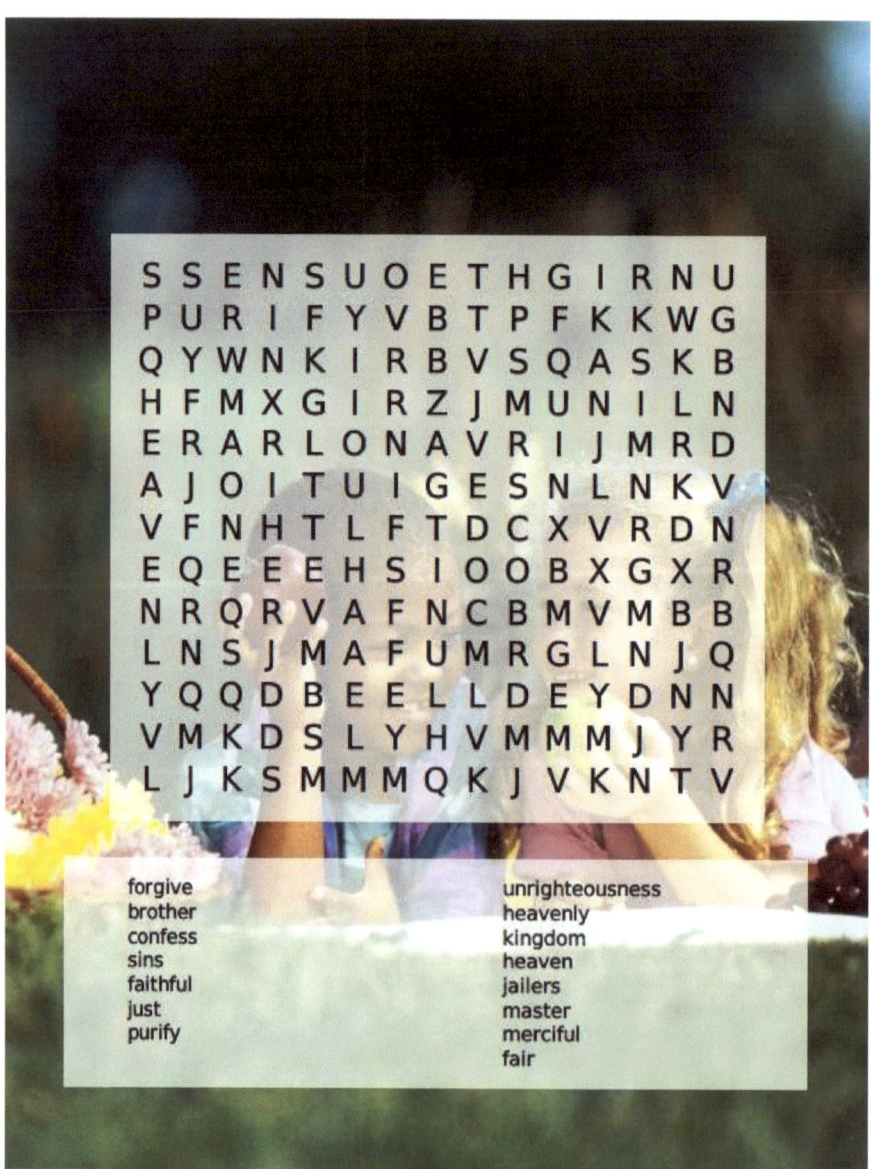

Journey of Faith Family Study Guide

Stage 4 - Life in God's Church

Lesson #12 - The Church

Bible Story

They devoted themselves to the apostles' teaching and to fellowship, to the breaking of bread and to prayer. Everyone was filled with awe at the many wonders and signs performed by the apostles. All the believers were together and had everything in common. They sold property and possessions to give to anyone who had need. Every day they continued to meet together in the temple courts. They broke bread in their homes and ate together with glad and sincere hearts, praising God and enjoying the favor of all the people. And the Lord added to their number daily those who were being saved. (Acts 2:42-47 NIV)

Children's Chat

i. *Who were the people in your story?*

   _____

   _____

ii. *What happens in the passage (story)?* The believers were _____ for the apostles' _____, _____, eating together, prayer and _____ God. They sold _____ and _____ to help each other. More people were being saved each <u>day</u>.

iii. *What does this story teach us about ourselves? God?* This story teaches us those God intends for the _____ members to grow relationally together.

Poem

There's life and death
That we must choose
There's hope or sorrow
For us to use
Sickness and pain lie in wait
But faith is waiting to determine our fate
Opposing forces all at work
You should choose to join the church
Or choose the world, and all its cares
Manipulated by the prince of air
Who lurks and searches for men to tempt
You and I are not exempt
Evil waits and works in men
To tease and please and draw you in
But there is help that will suffice
There's power in the body of Christ.
Join the church of God today
The kingdom awaits Christ is the way!

Journey of Faith Family Study Guide

Fun Activity

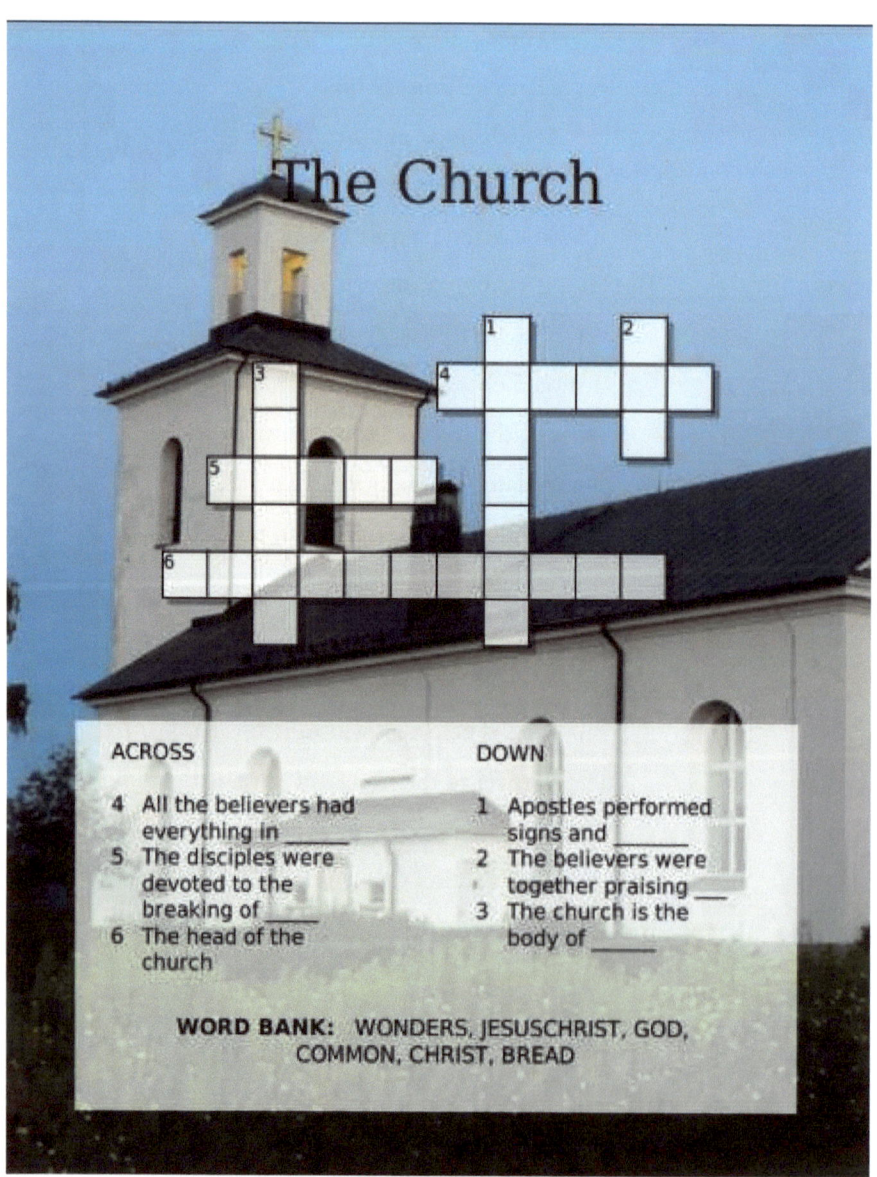

The Church

ACROSS
4 All the believers had everything in ___
5 The disciples were devoted to the breaking of ___
6 The head of the church

DOWN
1 Apostles performed signs and ___
2 The believers were together praising ___
3 The church is the body of ___

WORD BANK: WONDERS, JESUSCHRIST, GOD, COMMON, CHRIST, BREAD

Journey of Faith Family Study Guide

Lesson #13 - Baptism

Bible Story

Then Jesus came from Galilee to the Jordan to be baptized by John. But John tried to deter him, saying, "I need to be baptized by you, and do you come to me?" Jesus replied, "Let it be so now; it is proper for us to do this to fulfill all righteousness." Then John consented. As soon as Jesus was baptized, he went up out of the water. At that moment heaven was opened, and he saw the Spirit of God descending like a dove and alighting on him. And a voice from heaven said, "This is my Son, whom I love; with him I am well pleased." (Matthew 3:13-17 NIV)

Journey of Faith Family Study Guide

Children's Chat

i. *Who were the people in this story?*

   _____

   _____

ii. *What happened in this story?*

   John baptized _____. Heaven opened, and the Spirit of God _____ like a _____. God the Father spoke from heaven and said, "This is my <u>Son</u>, <u>Son</u> whom I _____; with him I am well _____."

iii. *What act of obedience is discussed?*

   John was obedient when he _____ Jesus.

   Jesus was _____ by being baptized.

iv. *What difficult decision is made or discussed?*

   John baptized Jesus even though he didn't feel _____ to do it.

v. *What does this story teach us about ourselves? God?*

   God honors _____.

Prayer

Father, teach us to follow the Lord Jesus, to obey your commands, surrender to your will, to fulfill your plan As we are baptized into the faith, through grace, Let all heaven and earth witness as we take a stand for Christ.

Journey of Faith Family Study Guide

Fun Activity

Baptism

ACROSS

1. Jesus was baptized by ___
4. The Spirit of God descended like a ___
5. A voice from ___ said, "This is my Son, whom I love"
6. John the ___

DOWN

2. Jesus was ___
3. John said, "I need to be baptized by ___"

WORD BANK: YOU, OBEDIENT, JOHN, HEAVEN, DOVE, BAPTIST

Journey of Faith Family Study Guide

Lesson #14 - Last Supper

Bible Story

On the first day of the Festival of Unleavened Bread, the disciples came to Jesus and asked, "Where do you want us to make preparations for you to eat the Passover?" [18] He replied, "Go into the city to a certain man and tell him, 'The Teacher says: My appointed time is near. I am going to celebrate the Passover with my disciples at your house.'" [19] So the disciples did as Jesus had directed them and prepared the Passover. [20] When evening came, Jesus was reclining at the table with the Twelve. (Matthew 26:17-20 NIV)

While they were eating, Jesus took bread, and when he had given thanks, he broke it and gave it to his disciples, saying, "Take and eat; this is my body." Then he took a cup, and when he had given thanks, he gave it to them, saying, "Drink from it, all of you. [28] This is my blood of the covenant, which is poured out for many for the forgiveness of sins. [29] I tell you, I will not drink from this fruit of the vine from now on until that day when I drink it new with you in my Father's kingdom." [30] When they had sung a hymn, they went out to the Mount of Olives. (Matthew 26:26-30 NIV)

Children's Chat

i. *Who were the people in this story?*

_____

_____

_____

ii. *What happened in this story?*
The disciples prepared the _____. While they were _____, Jesus took bread, gave _____, broke it and gave it to his _____, Then he took a cup, gave _____, they enjoyed the last _____, sung a hymn, and went out to the Mount of Olives.

iii. *What act of obedience is discussed?*
The disciples were obedient when they went into the city to a certain man and told him that _____ wanted to celebrate the Passover with the disciples at his _____.

iv. *Is there a promise of God discussed?*
Jesus promised fellowship with His disciples again in his Father's _____.

v. *What is God teaching us to do through this story?*
Jesus taught us to commit to the fellowship with other _____, through the Lord's _____, commemorating the body and _____ of Jesus.

Poem

When it's time to regenerate,

Time to let our spirits rise

For refreshing, and refocus on Christ alone

Our king sits enthroned

With glory and compassion to share

His love, Embroidered on our hearts, living there

We come to worship, leave to serve

Obeying, and we live unnerved

With steps divinely ordered above

We walk in the power of Jesus' blood

Then we return to resume our place

Before the throne, receiving grace

Let praise resound, as we sing

The body of the risen King!

Journey of Faith Family Study Guide

Fun Activity

Last Supper

ACROSS

2 Festival of Unleavened ____
3 this is my ____
5 do this in remembrance of ____
7 Jesus was _____ at the table

DOWN

1 Eat the ____
4 they had sung a ____
6 This is my ____ of the covenant, which is poured out
8 he broke it saying, "Take and ____"

WORD BANK: RECLINING, PASSOVER, ME, HYMN, EAT, BREAD, BODY, BLOOD

Journey of Faith Family Study Guide

Lesson #15 - Last Supper II

Bible Story

And while they were eating, he said, "Truly I tell you, one of you will betray me." [22] They were very sad and began to say to him one after the other, "Surely you don't mean me, Lord?" [23] Jesus replied, "The one who has dipped his hand into the bowl with me will betray me. [24] The Son of Man will go just as it is written about him. But woe to that man who betrays the Son of Man! It would be better for him if he had not been born." [25] Then Judas, the one who would betray him, said, "Surely you don't mean me, Rabbi?" Jesus answered, "You have said so." (Matthew 26:21-25 NIV)

Journey of Faith Family Study Guide

Children's Chat

i. *Who were the people in this story?*

_____

_____

_____

_____

ii. *What happened in this story?*

While they were eating, Jesus said, one of you will _____ me. They each asked if it were them. Jesus said it's the one who dipped his _____ _____ at the same time as Jesus. Jesus told _____ it was him.

iii. *What act of sin is discussed?*

_____ betrayed Jesus and turned Him in to the Roman Chief Priests to be _____.

iv. *What does this story teach us about ourselves? God?*

When Jesus said, "The Son of Man will go just as it is written about him", we learned that God's _____ must be fulfilled.

<u>Prayer</u>

Lord, preserve us for your salvation Let us unite in fellowship together, in suffering together, in service together, in persecution, in spiritual training and spiritual war together. Keep us from falling. Keep us near you.

Journey of Faith Family Study Guide

Fun Activity

Last Supper II

ACROSS

1. betrayed Jesus
5. woe to that ___ who betrays the Son of Man
6. Judas turned Jesus in to be _____

DOWN

2. the one who _____ his hand into the bowl
3. His heart was filled with ___
4. One of you will _____ me
5. betrayed for _____

WORD BANK: SIN, MONEY, MAN, JUDAS, DIPPED, BETRAY, ARRESTED

Journey of Faith Family Study Guide

Stage 5 - God's Scripture

Lesson #16 - Sacred Scripture I

Bible Story

Then Jesus was led by the Spirit into the wilderness to be tempted by the devil. After fasting forty days and forty nights, he was hungry. The tempter came to him and said, "If you are the Son of God, tell these stones to become bread." Jesus answered, "It is written: 'Man shall not live on bread alone, but on every word that comes from the mouth of God.'" (Matthew 4:1-4 NIV)

Journey of Faith Family Study Guide

Children's Chat

i. *Who were the people in this story?*

_____

_____

_____

_____

_____

ii. *What happened in this story?*

Jesus was led by the _____ into the _____. Jesus was tempted by the _____. Jesus fasted _____ days and nights. The devil tempted Jesus to turn the stones into _____. Jesus responded with the truth of the word of _____.

iii. *What sin or act of obedience is discussed?*

Jesus was obedient by resisting _____. He remembered, used, and acted on the _____ of God

i. *What difficult decision is made or discussed?*

The temptation was for Jesus to prove he was the _____ of God. To prove it, Jesus would have to show off his _____ for the devil. The difficult decision that Jesus made was to resist the spirit of pride.

iv. *What does this story teach us about ourselves? God?*

We learned that Jesus expects _____ to His word

A Prophetic Point

The Word has overcome the world. Get it in you before the world destroys you!

Prayer

Lord, our prayer is to be led by your word. Let our lives be directed by the light of your word, so we can live according to it. Strengthen us and preserve us according to every promise written in your word. Let your Holy name be praised!

Journey of Faith Family Study Guide

Fun Activity

Sacred Scripture

```
S D G N I T S A F L M
J S E R K N L P X R Q
R E E T E L I V E D Z
T B S N P T I R I P S
R G T U R M P N Y R L
J B O B S E E M Y N L
H U N G R Y D T E R Y
M L E P T E R L J T J
L R S G B O A X I J M
Q R R J F M Y D D W N
```

Jesus
Spirit
wilderness
tempted
devil

fasting
forty
hungry
tempter
stones
bread

Lesson #17 - Sacred Scripture II

Bible Story

Then the devil took him to the holy city and had him stand on the highest point of the temple. "If you are the Son of God," he said, "throw yourself down. For it is written: 'He will command his angels concerning you, and they will lift you up in their hands, so that you will not strike your foot against a stone.'" Jesus answered him, "It is also written: 'Do not put the Lord your God to the test.'" Again, the devil took him to a very high mountain and showed him all the kingdoms of the world and their splendor. "All this I will give you," he said, "if you will bow down and worship me." Jesus said to him, "Away from me, Satan! For it is written: 'Worship the Lord your God, and serve him only.'" Then the devil left him, and angels came and attended him. (Matthew 4:5-11 NIV)

Journey of Faith Family Study Guide

Children's Chat

i. *Who were the people in this story?*

_____

_____

ii. *What happened in this story?*

The devil took Jesus to the holy city and had him stand on the highest point of the temple and tempted Him to _____ to prove that God will send _____ to catch Him. Jesus told him "It is also written: 'Do not put the Lord your God _____.'"
Then the devil took him to a very high _____ and showed him all the kingdoms of the _____ and their splendor. He told Jesus to "bow down and worship me." But Jesus said "Away from me, Satan! For it is written: 'Worship the Lord your God, _____.'"

Then the _____ left him, and angels came and attended him.

iii. *What sin or act of obedience is discussed?*

Jesus was obedient to the Word of God which said, "do not put the Lord your God _____' "and 'Worship the Lord your God, _____.'"

iv. *What difficult decision is made or discussed?*

Jesus made the difficult decision of confronting the devil with the word of _____ (the sword) as His weapon.

v. *What does this story teach us about God?*

This story teaches us that God's word has authority over creation and evil _____.

Prayer

God, reveal the treasure in your holy word. Sensitize me to keep it in my heart. I want to remember, and obey your holy word. Bless me according to your perfect word. I want to be like Jesus. I want to know your word, see the truth in your word, and place my faith and hope in it so I am rewarded by it. For, your word will forever show me the way. Help me to understand what's right according to your word and I will forever praise your Holy name. Amen!

Journey of Faith Family Study Guide

Fun Activity

Sacred Scripture II

```
K E A N G E L S J T
I L S J V I K N O C
N P N P V Y I O O R
G M J E L A F M N W
D E D O T E M D O B
O T H N N A N R V Y
M L U O N T S D T J
S O T D E H K I O Z
M S Y S I Z C N M R
L R T P V R T M Z Y
```

devil
holy
city
temple
command
angels

foot
stone
test
mountain
kingdoms
splendor
worship

Journey of Faith Family Study Guide

Part II - Personal relationship with God

"The Season of Doing"

Journey of Faith Family Study Guide

Stage 6 - Walking in Grace

Journey of Faith Family Study Guide

Lesson #18 - Growing in grace

Bible Story

Every year Jesus' parents went to Jerusalem for the Festival of the Passover. When he was twelve years old, they went up to the festival, according to the custom. After the festival was over, while his parents were returning home, the boy Jesus stayed behind in Jerusalem, but they were unaware of it. Thinking he was in their company, they traveled on for a day. Then they began looking for him among their relatives and friends. When they did not find him, they went back to Jerusalem to look for him. After three days they found him in the temple courts, sitting among the teachers, listening to them and asking them questions. Everyone who heard him was amazed at his understanding and his answers. When his parents saw him, they were astonished. His mother said to him, "Son, why have you treated us like this? Your father and I have been anxiously searching for you." "Why were you searching for me?" he asked. "Didn't you know I had to be in my Father's house?" But they did not understand what he was saying to them. Then he went down to Nazareth with them and was obedient to them. But his mother treasured all these things in her heart. And Jesus grew in wisdom and stature, and in favor with God and man. (Luke 2:41-52 NIV)

Journey of Faith Family Study Guide

Children's Chat

i. *Who were the people in this story?*

ii. *What happened in this story? (List everything)*

iii. *What act of obedience is discussed?*

iv. *What difficult decision is made or discussed?*

v. *What does this story teach us about ourselves? God? -*

Journey of Faith Family Study Guide

Fun Activity

Growing in grace

```
P R N V M S P B M J R G W T P N Z N P T V
A R W T M T N W E R G I W J Y N D L Q Z R
S L M B T N J O Q B S J T T M X K Q Y Y Y
S W J R W L B Y I D G J E T Q D R W T Q J
O T L R Y N N G O T Y N J R E B V M P W M
V L D L B U T M N R S Q I L U B D N Q R B
E J J M M B N L J I J E E H Y S A Y N N Q
R J M T Q P G D S Y N V U P C Z A Z W O Q
S S E V I T A L E R A E F Q A R Q L B G A
T E A C H E R S S R E E T R E V A E E M D
R S Q Q B T S N T T S W E S N R D E A M L
U U G B T D Y M Y T N T S Y I I U Z S L T
O O R W N B O L I N H E A N E L E T T J D
C H L E K T T V Q F Q G R N A D G D A B R
L D I M S R A E A W P N T A D W Q P R T J
L R Y U M L L T Y M B B M R P I T Q D K S
F W C N N P H K W Y G M Q X M M N N L D W
Y X Q X M E M M B T N P V N J Z D G L N P
J D X E R V W M R K K D Q G B P Z T J V D
D D T M T Y B D M L Q J Z R Y M M N N Z X
```

parents
Jerusalem
Festival
Passover
custom traveled
relatives
friends
temple
courts
teachers
listening

questions
amazed
understanding
answers
searching
Father
house
Nazareth
obedient
grew
wisdom
stature

Journey of Faith Family Study Guide

Lesson #19 - Compassion for others

Bible Story

When Jesus heard what had happened, he withdrew by boat privately to a solitary place. Hearing of this, the crowds followed him on foot from the towns. When Jesus landed and saw a large crowd, he had compassion on them and healed their sick. As evening approached, the disciples came to him and said, "This is a remote place, and it's already getting late. Send the crowds away, so they can go to the villages and buy themselves some food." Jesus replied, "They do not need to go away. You give them something to eat." "We have here only five loaves of bread and two fish," they answered. "Bring them here to me," he said. And he directed the people to sit down on the grass. Taking the five loaves and the two fish and looking up to heaven, he gave thanks and broke the loaves. Then he gave them to the disciples, and the disciples gave them to the people. They all ate and were satisfied, and the disciples picked up twelve basketfuls of broken pieces that were left over. The number of those who ate was about five thousand men, besides women and children. (Matthew 14:13-21 NIV)

Journey of Faith Family Study Guide

Children's Chat

i. *Who were the people in this story?*

ii. *What happened in this story? (List everything)*

iii. *What difficult decision is made or discussed?*

iv. *Is there a promise of God discussed?*

v. *What does this story teach us about ourselves? God? -*

Journey of Faith Family Study Guide

Fun Activity

Journey of Faith Family Study Guide

Stage 7 - Daily Deliverance

Journey of Faith Family Study Guide

Lesson #20 - Liberation

Bible Story

But now, this is what the LORD says he who created you, Jacob, he who formed you, Israel: "Do not fear, for I have redeemed you; I have summoned you by name; you are mine. When you pass through the waters, I will be with you; and when you pass through the rivers, they will not sweep over you. When you walk through the fire, you will not be burned; the flames will not set you ablaze. For I am the LORD your God, the Holy One of Israel, your Savior; I give Egypt for your ransom, Cush and Seba in your stead. Since you are precious and honored in my sight, and because I love you, I will give people in exchange for you, nations in exchange for your life. Do not be afraid, for I am with you; I will bring your children from the east and gather you from the west. I will say to the north, 'Give them up!' and to the south, 'Do not hold them back.' Bring my sons from afar and my daughters from the ends of the earth - everyone who is called by my name, whom I created for my glory, whom I formed and made." (Isaiah 43:1-7 NIV)

Children's Chat

i. *Who is the writer of the passage?*

ii. *What happened in this story? (List everything)*

iii. *What difficult decision is made or discussed?*

iv. *Is there a promise of God discussed?*

v. *What does this story teach us about ourselves? God?*

Journey of Faith Family Study Guide

Fun Activity

Journey of Faith Family Study Guide

Lesson #21 – Rescued

Bible Story

So the king gave the order, and they brought Daniel and threw him into the lions' den. The king said to Daniel, "May your God, whom you serve continually, rescue you!" A stone was brought and placed over the mouth of the den, and the king sealed it with his own signet ring and with the rings of his nobles, so that Daniel's situation might not be changed. Then the king returned to his palace and spent the night without eating and without any entertainment being brought to him. And he could not sleep. At the first light of dawn, the king got up and hurried to the lions' den. When he came near the den, he called to Daniel in an anguished voice, "Daniel, servant of the living God, has your God, whom you serve continually, been able to rescue you from the lions?" Daniel answered, "May the king live forever! My God sent his angel, and he shut the mouths of the lions. They have not hurt me, because I was found innocent in his sight. Nor have I ever done any wrong before you, Your Majesty." The king was overjoyed and gave orders to lift Daniel out of the den. And when Daniel was lifted from the den, no wound was found on him, because he had trusted in his God. At the king's command, the men who had falsely accused Daniel were brought in and thrown into the lions' den, along with their wives and children. And before they reached the floor of the den, the lions overpowered them and crushed all their bones. (Daniel 6:16-24 NIV)

Children's Chat

i. *Who were the people in this story?*

   _____

   _____

ii. *What happened in this story? (List everything)*

   _____

   _____

   _____

   _____

iii. *Is there a promise of God discussed?*

   _____

   _____

iv. *What does this story teach us about ourselves? God?*

   _____

   _____

Journey of Faith Family Study Guide

Fun Activity

Rescued

```
D D H S E A L E D K W E
A E E U L C W T I B U B
J N R Y R J R N U C X F
J N G E O R G U S H A X
T E L E W J I E S L S W
R N D E L O R E S H B T
U O E M I N P E D M E S
S T S C T N L R V G N D
T S U E O Y A K E O O D
E D C P N N L D I V E D
D B C L J O N L T N O G
B M A D D R B I G N T B
```

king   angel
Daniel   shut
lions   innocent
den   overjoyed
God   trusted
rescue   falsely
stone   accused
sealed   overpowered
hurried   crushed
              bones

Journey of Faith Family Study Guide

Lesson #22 - Saved for others' sake

Bible Story

Then King Darius wrote to all the nations and peoples of every language in all the earth: "May you prosper greatly! "I issue a decree that in every part of my kingdom people must fear and reverence the God of Daniel. "For he is the living God and he endures forever; his kingdom will not be destroyed, his dominion will never end. He rescues and he saves; he performs signs and wonders in the heavens and on the earth. He has rescued Daniel from the power of the lions." So Daniel prospered during the reign of Darius and the reign of Cyrus the Persian. (Daniel 6:35-38)

Children's Chat

1. *Who were the people in this story?*

   _____
   _____
   _____

2. *What happened in this story? (List everything)*

   _____
   _____
   _____
   _____
   _____

   What does this story teach us about ourselves? God?

   _____
   _____
   _____

   Is there a promise of God discussed?

   _____
   _____
   _____
   _____

Journey of Faith Family Study Guide

Fun Activity

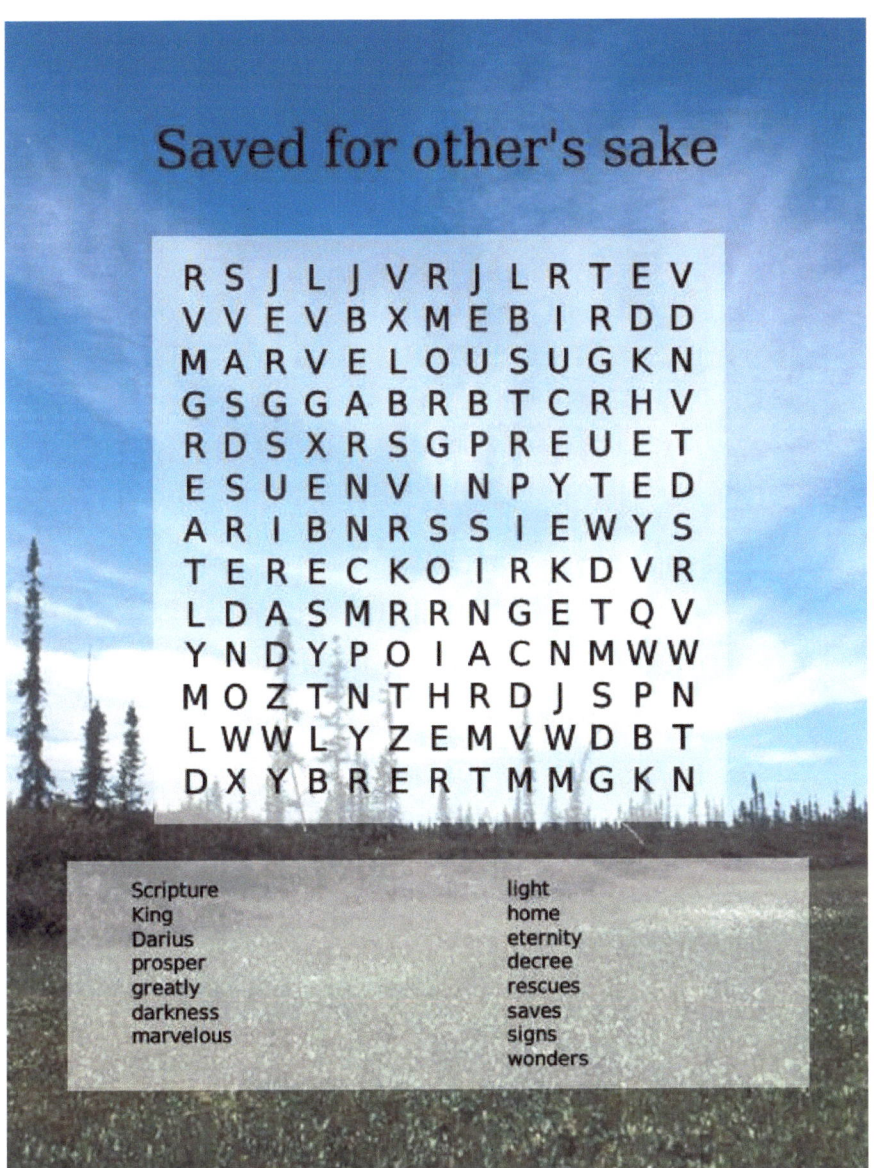

Lesson #23 - *"Restored"*

Bible Story

Early in the morning, Jesus stood on the shore, but the disciples did not realize that it was Jesus. He called out to them, "Friends, haven't you any fish?" "No," they answered. He said, "Throw your net on the right side of the boat and you will find some." When they did, they were unable to haul the net in because of the large number of fish. Then the disciple whom Jesus loved said to Peter, "It is the Lord!" As soon as Simon Peter heard him say, "It is the Lord," he wrapped his outer garment around him (for he had taken it off) and jumped into the water. The other disciples followed in the boat, towing the net full of fish, for they were not far from shore, about a hundred yards. When they landed, they saw a fire of burning coals there with fish on it, and some bread. Jesus said to them, "Bring some of the fish you have just caught." So Simon Peter climbed back into the boat and dragged the net ashore. It was full of large fish, 153, but even with so many the net was not torn. Jesus said to them, "Come and have breakfast." None of the disciples dared ask him, "Who are you?" They knew it was the Lord. Jesus came, took the bread and gave it to them, and did the same with the fish. This was now the third time Jesus appeared to his disciples after he was raised from the dead. (John 21:1-14 NIV)

Children's Chat

i. *Who were the people in this story?*

_____

_____

_____

ii. *What happened in this story? (List everything)*

_____

_____

_____

_____

iii. *What act of obedience is discussed?*

_____

_____

_____

_____

iv. *What difficult decision is made or discussed?*

_____

_____

_____

_____

v. *What does this story teach us about God?*

_____

_____

_____

_____

_____

Journey of Faith Family Study Guide

Fun Activity

Journey of Faith Family Study Guide

Stage 8 - Developing Discipline

Journey of Faith Family Study Guide

Lesson #24 - "Fasting & Prayer"

Bible Story

And when you pray, do not be like the hypocrites, for they love to pray standing in the synagogues and on the street corners to be seen by others. Truly I tell you, they have received their reward in full. But when you pray, go into your room, close the door and pray to your Father, who is unseen. Then your Father, who sees what is done in secret, will reward you. And when you pray, do not keep on babbling like pagans, for they think they will be heard because of their many words. Do not be like them, for your Father knows what you need before you ask him. "This, then, is how you should pray: "'Our Father in heaven, hallowed be your name, your kingdom come, your will be done, on earth as it is in heaven. Give us today our daily bread. And forgive us our debts, as we also have forgiven our debtors. And lead us not into temptation, but deliver us from the evil one.' (Matthew 6:5-13 NIV)

Children's Chat

i.   *Who were the people in this story?*

_____
_____
_____

ii.   *What happened in this story? (List everything)*

_____
_____
_____
_____
_____
_____

iii.   *What sin or act of obedience is discussed?*

_____
_____
_____

iv.   *What are we being taught to do?*

_____
_____
_____

v.   *What does this story teach us about ourselves? God?*

_____
_____
_____

Prayer

Lord, help us to develop our own private, intimate and personal relationship with you. Build it on our trust in you. We know that you know everything about us and that only you can help us. Lord, help our family depend on you.

Journey of Faith Family Study Guide

Fun Activity

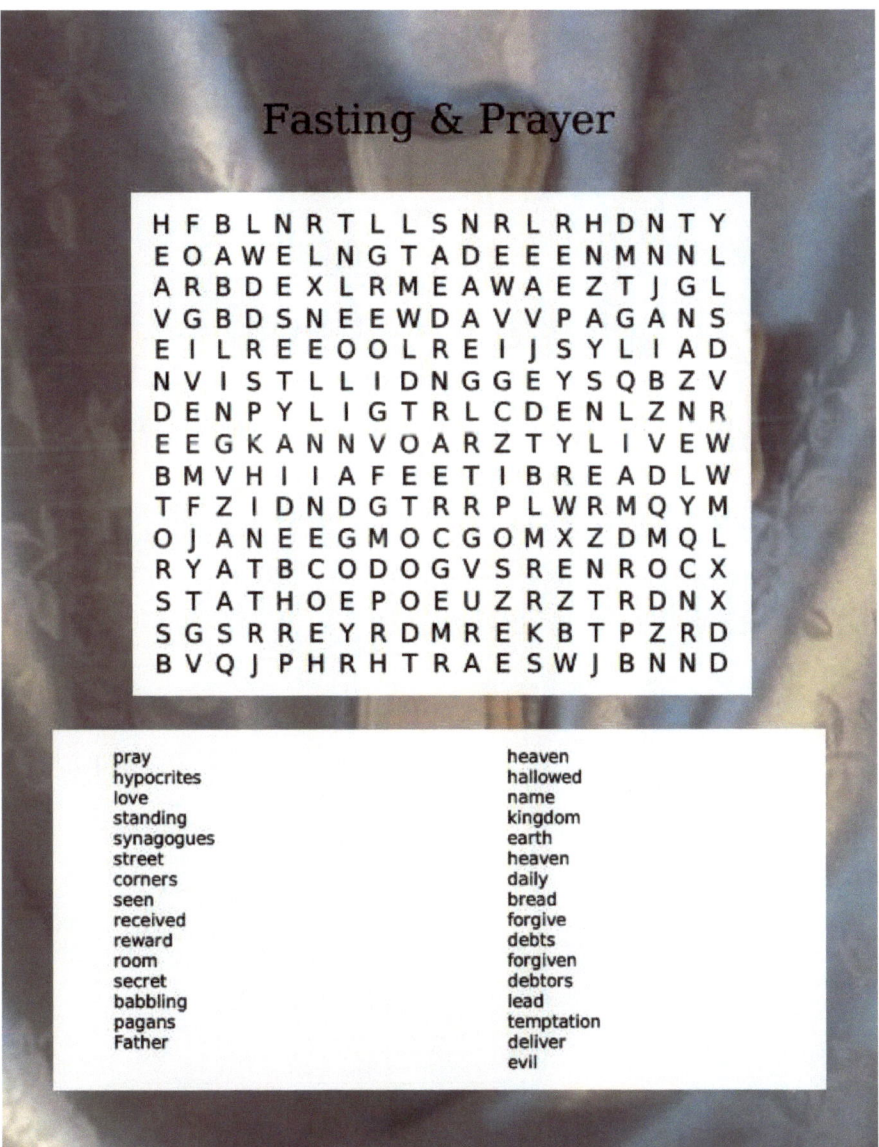

Journey of Faith Family Study Guide

Lesson #25 - "Praise & Worship"

Bible Story

Come, let us sing for joy to the LORD; let us shout aloud to the Rock of our salvation. Let us come before him with thanksgiving and extol him with music and song. For the LORD is the great God, the great King above all gods. In his hand are the depths of the earth, and the mountain peaks belong to him. The sea is his, for he made it, and his hands formed the dry land. Come, let us bow down in worship, let us kneel before the LORD our Maker; for he is our God and we are the people of his pasture, the flock under his care. (Psalm 95:1-7 NIV)

Children's Chat

i. *Who is the author of the story?*

ii. *What happened in this story? (List everything)*

iii. *What sin or act of obedience is discussed?*

iv. *What does this story teach us about God?*

v. *What does this story teach us about ourselves?*

Journey of Faith Family Study Guide

Poem

We come singing, shouting
We start kneeling and bowing

Our hearts move into worship of the Lord our God
When we focus on you

We praise you for all you've done
And we hope in the things you will do

We live to serve the King of Kings -
Who reigns with dominion and power

In our hearts, sweet melodies ring
Until your glory showers
Amen

Journey of Faith Family Study Guide

Fun Activity

Lesson #26 - "Service & Fellowship"

They preached the gospel in that city and won a large number of disciples. Then they returned to Lystra, Iconium and Antioch, strengthening the disciples and encouraging them to remain true to the faith. "We must go through many hardships to enter the kingdom of God," they said. Paul and Barnabas appointed elders for them in each church and, with prayer and fasting, committed them to the Lord, in whom they had put their trust. After going through Pisidia, they came into Pamphylia, and when they had preached the word in Perga, they went down to Attalia. From Attalia they sailed back to Antioch, where they had been committed to the grace of God for the work they had now completed. On arriving there, they gathered the church together and reported all that God had done through them and how he had opened a door of faith to the Gentiles. And they stayed there a long time with the disciples. (Acts 14:21-28 NIV)

Journey of Faith Family Study Guide

Children's Chat

i. Who were the people in this story?

ii. What happened in this story? (List everything)

iii. Is there a promise of God discussed?

iv. What are we being taught to do?

vi. What does this story teach us about ourselves? God?

Journey of Faith Family Study Guide

Poem

Our leaders walk with the Lord
They study, pray, and proclaim the truth
Then extend invitations to discipleship
And to join the kingdom with you

They encourage us all to stay committed
And endure the hard times we hate
This is how God builds the ministry
To assist our journey of faith

God calls men and women
And reveals whose been called
They are disciplined, and prepared in advance,
Strengthened to overcome a fall

Strengthened to fight the enemy
Strengthened not to quit
Strengthened infinitely
To be spiritually fit

With prayer and fasting, they are later chosen
And appointed somewhere to serve
We all share the gospel outside
And to support other Christians in the church
This is the service in the ministry Amen!

Journey of Faith Family Study Guide

Fun Activity

Journey of Faith Family Study Guide

Stage 9 - Loving obedience

Journey of Faith Family Study Guide

Lesson #27 - Love I

Bible Story

Hearing that Jesus had silenced the Sadducees, the Pharisees got together. One of them, an expert in the law, tested him with this question: "Teacher, which is the greatest commandment in the Law?" Jesus replied: "'Love the Lord your God with all your heart and with all your soul and with all your mind. This is the first and greatest commandment. And the second is like it: 'Love your neighbor as yourself.' All the Law and the Prophets hang on these two commandments." (Matthew 22:34-39 NIV)

Children's Chat

i. *Who were the people in this story?*

ii. *What happened in this story? (List everything)*

iii. *What sin or act of obedience is discussed?*

iv. *What does this story teach us about ourselves? God?*

Prayer

Heavenly Father, teach us to love you, your people. You have a way of creating people the way they are, accepting them where they are, and developing them into who they are supposed to become. Help us to see others through your eyes and love them as much as possible. Amen!

Journey of Faith Family Study Guide

Fun Activity

109

Journey of Faith Family Study Guide

Lesson #28 - Love II

Bible Story

And now these three remain: faith, hope and love. But the greatest of these is love. (1 Corinthians 13:13)

Children's Chat

i. *Who is the author of the scripture?*

_____

_____

ii. *What are we being taught to do?*

_____

_____

_____

_____

iii. *What does this story teach us about ourselves? God?*

_____

_____

_____

Poem

Faith unlocks the door
Hope sees what's on the other side
Love holds my agenda, my relationships, my destiny, and the will of God for my life

Journey of Faith Family Study Guide

Fun Activity

Journey of Faith Family Study Guide

Lesson #29 - Obedience

Scripture

"Before long, the world will not see me anymore, but you will see me. Because I live, you also will live. On that day you will realize that I am in my Father, and you are in me, and I am in you. [21] Whoever has my commands and keeps them is the one who loves me. The one who loves me will be loved by my Father, and I too will love them and show myself to them." John 14:19-21

Children's Chat

1. *Who were the people in this story?*

   _____

   _____

2. *What sin or act of obedience is discussed?*

   _____

   _____

3. *Is there a promise of God discussed?*

   _____

   _____

4. *What does this story teach us about ourselves? God?*

   _____

   _____

   _____

Poem

Who can see me?

Others cannot see me

But you can

Who is in me?

Others are not in me

But you are

Who is in Christ?

I live in Christ

Since you are in me, you will live in Christ

Who is in the Father?

Since I am in the father and you are in me, then you are in the father

Who is in you?

Since the Holy Spirit is in you, then I am inside of you, and the father too

Who loves me?

Whoever is in me, loves me

You must obey me to be in me

If you obey me, then you love me

Who loves you?

I love you.

Love me and I will love you more

Our father will love you

We will live in you and love you even more

Journey of Faith Family Study Guide

Fun Activity

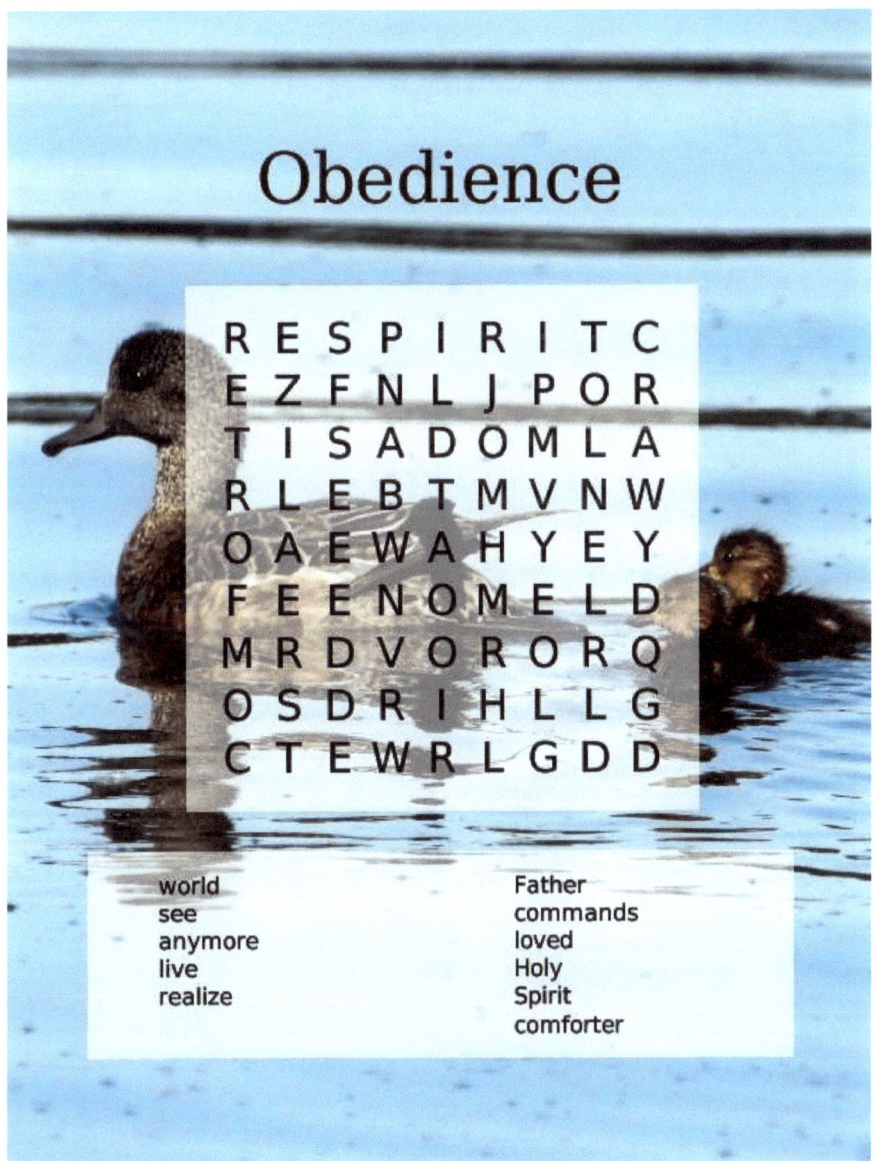

Journey of Faith Family Study Guide

Stage 10 - Suffering Affliction

Journey of Faith Family Study Guide

Lesson #30 - Suffering

Bible Story

For those who are led by the Spirit of God are the children of God. The Spirit you received does not make you slaves, so that you live in fear again; rather, the Spirit you received brought about your adoption to sonship. And by him we cry, *"Abba,* Father." The Spirit himself testifies with our spirit that we are God's children. Now if we are children, then we are heirs—heirs of God and co-heirs with Christ, if indeed we share in his sufferings in order that we may also share in his glory. (Romans 8:14-17 NIV)

Journey of Faith Family Study Guide

Children's Chat

    i.   *Who is the author of the text?*

    _____

    _____

    ii.   *What sin or act of obedience is discussed?*

    _____

    _____

    _____

    iii.   *Is there a promise of God discussed?*

    _____

    _____

    _____

    iv.   *What does this story teach us about God?*

    _____

    _____

    _____

    v.   *What does this story teach us about ourselves?*

    _____

    _____

    _____

Journey of Faith Family Study Guide

<u>Prayer</u>

Father, send your spirit to fill us again
Remind us that Jesus is a friend.
Let us follow the way
Obey and do what the spirit say
Children of the King,
Accept our prayer
Teach us to walk and live as heirs

Journey of Faith Family Study Guide

Fun Activity

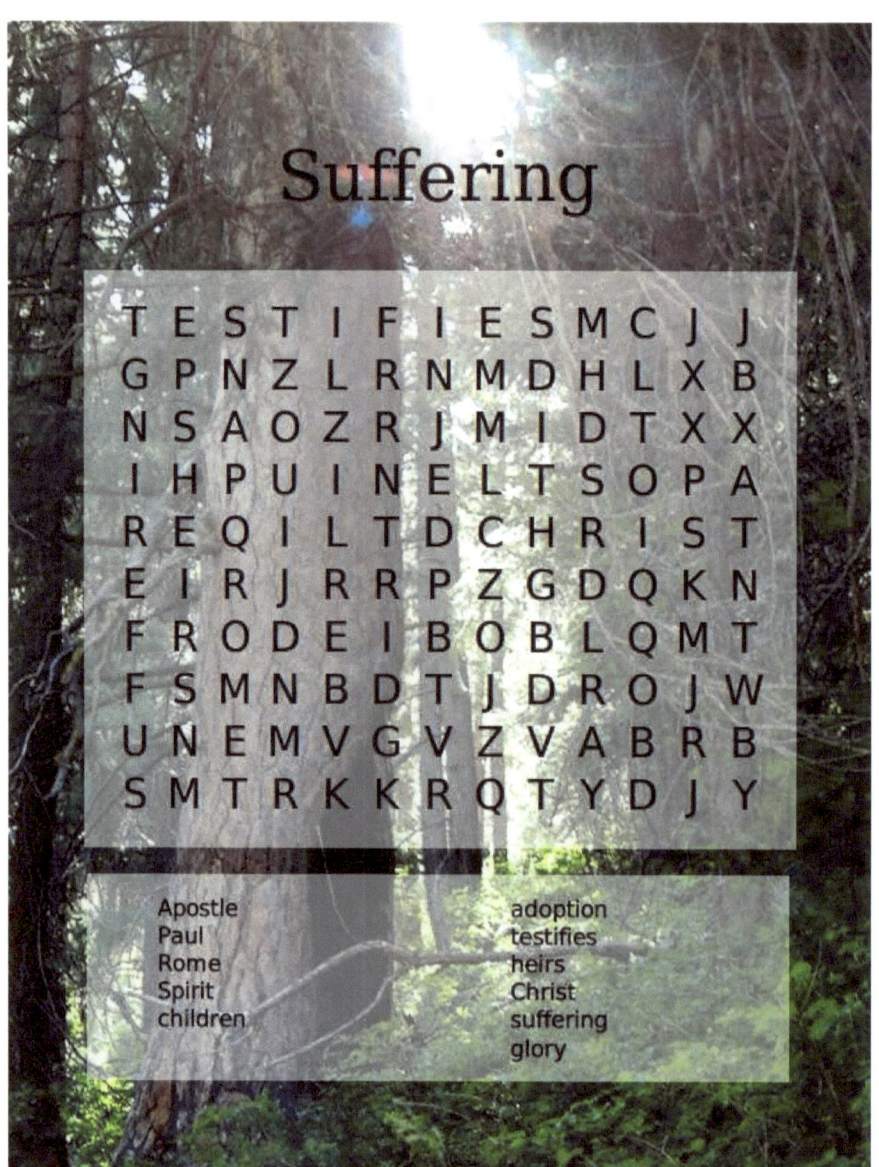

Journey of Faith Family Study Guide

Lesson #31 - Maturity & Resilience

Bible Story

You, however, know all about my teaching, my way of life, my purpose, faith, patience, love, endurance, persecutions, sufferings—what kinds of things happened to me in Antioch, Iconium and Lystra, the persecutions I endured. Yet the Lord rescued me from all of them. In fact, everyone who wants to live a godly life in Christ Jesus will be persecuted, while evildoers and impostors will go from bad to worse, deceiving and being deceived. But as for you, continue in what you have learned and have become convinced of, because you know those from whom you learned it, and how from infancy you have known the Holy Scriptures, which are able to make you wise for salvation through faith in Christ Jesus. All Scripture is God-breathed and is useful for teaching, rebuking, correcting and training in righteousness, so that the servant of God may be thoroughly equipped for every good work. (2 timothy 3:10-17)

Journey of Faith Family Study Guide

Children's Chat

i. *Who were the people in this story?*

ii. *What happened in this story? (List everything)*

iii. *Is there a promise of God discussed?*

iv. *What are we being told to do?*

v. *What does this story teach us about ourselves?*

vi. *What does this story teach us about God?*

Poem

You know my way
What God requires

The truth I teach
How I aspire

The way I live
And handle stress

The faith in me
That keeps me blessed

The way I wait,
How I go through

These things
I expect of you

In life you'll often see the mark
Then you'll seem so far apart

If you should fall and start to thirst
Go back to what you've learned at first

A holy God saved sinful you
When you had no chance, had no clue

He called your name, reached out His hand
And saved you from the sinking sand

Just call His name again my friend
He will return, remove your sin

Heal your soul, restore your life
He'll do it once, do it twice

Just recall the sacrifice -
It's of the Lord who is the Christ

The cross, the blood
The will of God, eternal love

All worked for you
Now you should know

You can bounce back
You will grow

Seek the Lord in love, in Haste
Salvation comes to those with faith!

Journey of Faith Family Study Guide

Fun Activity

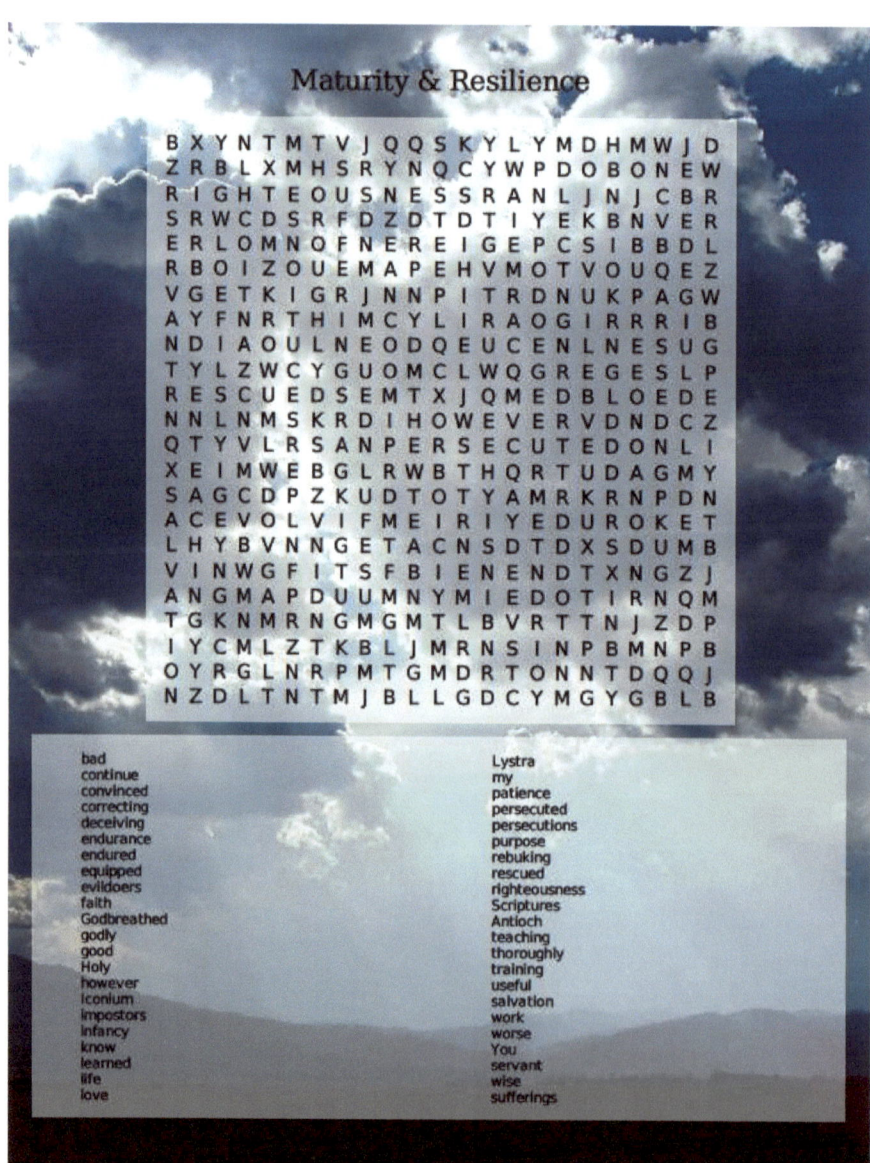

Journey of Faith Family Study Guide

Stage 11 – Glory

Journey of Faith Family Study Guide

Lesson #32 - The Glory of God

Bible Story

Praise be to the God and Father of our Lord Jesus Christ, who has blessed us in the heavenly realms with every spiritual blessing in Christ. For he chose us in him before the creation of the world to be holy and blameless in his sight. In love he predestined us for adoption to sonship through Jesus Christ, in accordance with his pleasure and will— to the praise of his glorious grace, which he has freely given us in the one he loves. In him we have redemption through his blood, the forgiveness of sins, in accordance with the riches of God's grace that he lavished on us. With all wisdom and understanding, he made known to us the mystery of his will according to his good pleasure, which he purposed in Christ, to be put into effect when the times reach their fulfillment—to bring unity to all things in heaven and on earth under Christ. In him we were also chosen, having been predestined according to the plan of him who works out everything in conformity with the purpose of his will, in order that we, who were the first to put our hope in Christ, might be for the praise of his glory. And you also were included in Christ when you heard the message of truth, the gospel of your salvation. When you believed, you were marked in him with a seal, the promised Holy Spirit, who is a deposit guaranteeing our inheritance until the redemption of those who are God's possession—to the praise of his glory. (Ephesians 1:3-14 NIV)

Children's Chat

i. *Who were the people in this story?*

ii. *Is there a promise of God discussed?*

iii. *What does this story teach us about ourselves?*

iv. *What does this story teach us about God?*

Poem

The God of heaven has a blessing to share

It is a spiritual gift, it is truly rare

It is for those who have faith,

Who'll become holy?

Children, adopted by grace

It's time to get it, just hope for it, you'll feel it

If you're sealed with the Spirit, then God will reveal it.

We have a trust fund worth of gifts of God

He will let us redeem them in time.

Journey of Faith Family Study Guide

Fun Activity

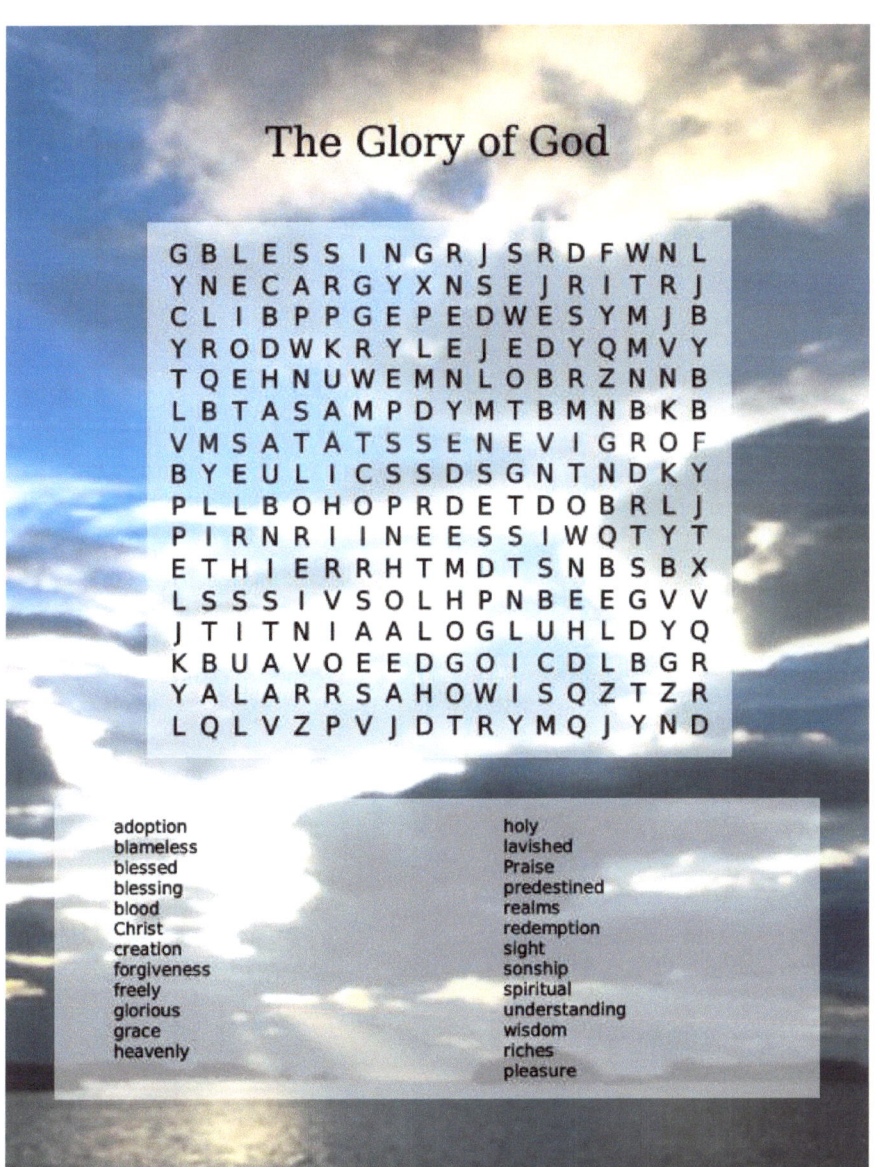

Journey of Faith Family Study Guide

Lesson #33 - Christ formed in you

Bible Story

Now I rejoice in what I am suffering for you, and I fill up in my flesh what is still lacking in regard to Christ's afflictions, for the sake of his body, which is the church. I have become its servant by the commission God gave me to present to you the word of God in its fullness— the mystery that has been kept hidden for ages and generations, but is now disclosed to the Lord's people. To them God has chosen to make known among the Gentiles the glorious riches of this mystery, which is Christ in you, the hope of glory. He is the one we proclaim, admonishing and teaching everyone with all wisdom, so that we may present everyone fully mature in Christ. To this end I strenuously contend with all the energy Christ so powerfully works in me. (Colossians 1:24-29 NIV)

Children's Chat

i. *Who is the author of the text?*

ii. *Who were the people in this story?*

iii. *What happened in this story? (List everything)*

iv. *What sin or act of obedience is discussed?*

v. *What difficult decision is made or discussed?*

vi. *Is there a promise of God discussed?*

_____
_____
_____
_____

vii. *What does this story teach us God?*

_____
_____
_____
_____

Journey of Faith Family Study Guide

Fun Activity

Poem

The Lord prepares preachers to proclaim the word of God

The word is rich and full to mature the church at large

The truth of God proclaimed, the mystery, Christ in you

To build us up, to encourage and to mature us too

The servants suffer, agonize, but rejoice along the way

Working diligently to serve the church and see the mighty day

To see the goal, you made whole

That's what ends the story

Christ in you, will unfold

That's the hope of glory

ABOUT THE AUTHOR

Dr. Derrick L Randolph, Sr. is from Baltimore, Maryland.

www.ingramcontent.com/pod-product-compliance
Lightning Source LLC
Chambersburg PA
CBHW041801160426
43191CB00001B/2